BRITAIN IN OLD PHOTOGRAPHS

Teddington, Twickenham & The Hamptons

Past & Present

Garth Groombridge

First published in 2007 by
Sutton Publishing

Reprinted in 2011 by
The History Press
The Mill, Brimscombe Port,
Stroud, Gloucestershire, GL5 1RW
www.thehistorypress.co.uk

Copyright © Garth Groombridge, 2011

British Library Cataloguing in Publication Data
A catalogue record for this book is available from the British Library.

ISBN 978-0-7509-4587-5

Typeset in 10.5/13.5pt Photina.
Typesetting and origination by
Sutton Publishing Limited.
Printed and bound in England.

With thanks for the help, assistance and additional research carried out by members of the Borough of Twickenham Local History Society, the Local Studies Library at Richmond Town Hall, the Hampton and Teddington Societies, and others.

In memory of my mother, Bessie Emma Watson, née Anderson, 1919–2008

Contents

Acknowledgements   4

Introduction   7

1. Teddington   11
2. Twickenham   57
3. The Hamptons   91

Afterword   127

ACKNOWLEDGEMENTS

I should like to thank all those who helped in identifying and researching the photographs, and in supplying historical information and background. In particular, I would like to thank Ken Howe and John Sheaf of the Borough of Twickenham Local History Society. Ken was instrumental in putting me in contact with Simon Fletcher at Sutton Publishing, and so he is the initial spark behind this book. John Sheaf has been absolutely invaluable, not only in helping to correctly identify some of my photographs, but also in providing extremely useful historical information for the Hampton and Hampton Hill area and comments on the text. Likewise, Tony Beckles Willson was very helpful in researching and identifying a number of photographs of Twickenham.

At the Teddington Society I should like to thank Mary Green, who sent me P.A. Ching's book, *The Houses in Teddington 1800 to 2000 AD*, which provided me with additional historical information of the High Street and Park Road. Paddy Ching also kindly gave me further information, dates and history on various shops and houses in Teddington, for which again I am very grateful.

At the Hampton Society I should like to thank John Farndon and Jean Alen. Jean, in turn, recommended Terry Pearson, who offered to identify and research my photographs of the Hampton Nursery Lands, and Hampton Hill High Street.

Tony Hillman was extremely energetic and helpful in initially identifying Nursery Land sites around Oak Avenue, and taking and sending me photographs which, later, I could use as a guide for my own photographs.

Luke Denison and Nik Pollard, of the Local History Studies Library at the Old Town Hall in Richmond, have been especially invaluable in helping to trace, confirm or uncover shop names in Teddington and Twickenham during this period, as well as supplying other interesting facts concerning the historical background of such businesses, newspaper articles and the Nursery Lands exhibition.

In addition I should like to thank Neal Chapman for identifying some of the Twickenham photographs and for information about Colne Road (or 'Back Lane' as it was once known) and the Green; the Maple Leaf pharmacist for his information about his shop and his immediate neighbours; Jane Rees and Mrs Patricia White, the Archivist for Lady Eleanor Holles School, Hampton Hill, for information concerning Burlington House, Uxbridge Road; Mr Alec Wallace and Mr Pearce, who both supplied very useful information about their respective properties and localities in Twickenham; and Carlie Lipscombe for information on St John's Hospital.

Henry Harrison outlined the recent history of the Eel Pie Island boatyards; while Stella Gheury de Bray, Membership Secretary of the Mary Wallace Theatre, helped with information about the old Mission Hall. Bill Weisblatt, of Richmond Borough Mind, sent me information about Centre 32, one of the three shops in Hampton Road, Twickenham; Alex Gardner answered my questions about Gardinia Lodge, Old Farm Road; as did Kara Godfrey about Houghton, in Oak Avenue. Steve Prior of Townend's estate agency and Claire Gilles from Dexter's, as well as the staff at Chase Buchanan, all responded to my queries about current house prices in Twickenham.

I should like to thank Ralph Cox and his colleagues at the Twickenham Museum who were extremely helpful to my general enquiries about Twickenham, and who again enabled me to pinpoint several photograph locations. I should also like to thank Samantha Edgar and Richard Hands, at Churcham House, Teddington, for answering my email enquiries, even though they were unable to help me. I should also like to thank the various correspondents of the online VOX POP who contributed information or encouragement, notably Ken Elmes and Geoff Dadswell for Twickenham, and Councillor James Mumford for Teddington.

The author in the 1970s.

With this second edition I would like to thank former Teddington residents Graham Barrett and the late Tom Clark for correcting my mistake that the July 1944 Church Road bomb was a V1, not a V2, and Graham for his recollections concerning Church Lane. I also wish to thank Lucy Childs for the fascinating information she gave me concerning Albion Road and the Old Coach House, Twickenham.

Unfortunately, not all the information supplied could be incorporated into the text, but where possible I have passed the data on to local historians.

Finally, I wish to thank all those unnamed people to whom I spoke during my research trips to Teddington, Twickenham and Hampton, and the owners and occupants of all the houses and property I have photographed, both thirty years ago and in the last year.

All photographs were taken by the author.

Linda's hair fashion, 63 Richmond Road, Twickenham, and the gateway of and part of the Mulberry Tree public house on the right.

Nos 59–63 Richmond Road, 2006. No. 61 appears to be a private residence, while no. 63 is now Salon #1, and at no. 65 the old Mulberry Tree has now become The Clubhouse, which has been run by the former landlord of The White Swan on Twickenham Riverside since 2002. It is now a pub-restaurant that offers real ale, home-made food, a friendly atmosphere and even a floodlit and secluded 'secret garden'.

INTRODUCTION

From early childhood until my early thirties, when I finally moved away – first to Sunbury, then in 1985 Southampton – I lived in various locations in Teddington, Hampton Hill, Teddington again, then Twickenham. Of the three, Teddington was the place which I regarded as my home town. It was where my mother's family had lived and where my maternal grandparents, including various uncles and aunts, are buried, in Teddington Cemetery, in Church Road. My mother's maiden name was Anderson and her father, John Stuart Anderson, was a professional nurseryman or landscape-gardener; although during and after the First World War my grandmother also had a grocer's shop, located in Walpole Road, apparently between Walpole Place and Broad Street. My grandparents had lived at what had been 100 Church Road, opposite what is now the new school – all of these places were destroyed in July 1944 by a V1 rocket-bomb. By that time grandfather Anderson had already died. According to my mother he was a gentle man, who – having barely survived the horrors of the First World War – was appalled by another terrible war in which at least three of his sons (my uncles Jack, George and Leslie) went off to fight. The family legend has it that when the bomb took out the house in Church Road (along with what was then Argyll Road and parts of Somerset Road), my grandmother had hidden under the stairs, and was fortunate enough to survive, comparatively unharmed, as the house itself collapsed around her.

I was born at Hampton Court, which always sounds more impressive than it really was. In those dreary, immediate postwar years before the National Health Service was established, I was born – like a number of others of my generation – at the Bearsted Memorial Hospital, which later became Rotary Court. After my parents divorced I lived with my grandmother and mother's unmarried brother in Somerset Road, no. 20 as it was, one of the postwar prefabs constructed to 'temporarily' house the bombed-out residents, supposedly for eighteen months, but where they continued to live until the early 1960s. The site is now occupied by 10 Argyle House, immediately next to Stuart Grove. Later I lived briefly with my mother and stepfather in an upstairs flat at 27 Walpole Road, before moving to Windmill Road, Hampton Hill. A few years later we moved again, this time to 10 Cross Street, just off Hampton Hill High Street, which had been where my stepfather's mother had lived. It was a two-up two-down cottage, with no bathroom and an outside loo. Some years previously he had bought it for (I believe) the princely sum of £125, as a security for her old age – plus another £25 for an extra bit of back garden.

We lived there until I was in my mid-teens, when we moved again, this time to 3A Fairfax Road, near the Kingston Road. Here I stayed until after I was married in 1970;

then my first wife and I moved to Bolton Gardens. A few years later, in either 1975 or 1976, we bought our first house, 47 Warwick Road, Twickenham, which is where we lived until our marriage broke up in 1981, and I moved, first to Sunbury, then Ashford, then Southampton.

It was during this period that a combined interest in history, architecture and photography ignited my life-long pursuit of taking photographs of old or interesting houses or buildings, the results of which form the basis of this collection, mostly dating from the 1970s. Unfortunately, good intentions are not enough. In retrospect, my local photography was neither systematic nor complete. I did not always properly record dates or location (something that now, over thirty years later, creates problems with identification), while, again looking back now from the vantage of mature middle age, I am both amazed and puzzled by my apparent selectivity and omissions. Much was photographed, but as much again was not, and often the places that were the most familiar were the likeliest to be forgotten or neglected. Another serious limitation in the earliest (and, by default, most interesting) photographs was in the nature of the camera – a small Kodak Instamatic: very basic, with good-quality pictures reliant on sun or bright light. Only later, in the mid-1970s, did I start to use a 35mm Praktica camera that was more flexible in varied lighting conditions. But again, unfortunately, with the new, better camera I did not attempt to duplicate those photographs taken with the Kodak that had been too dark. My only excuse is that I was only in my twenties and easily distracted by other things.

The result is rather like reading a book of which some of the pages are stuck together. The reader, like the one of *this* book, cannot help wonder what he or she might have missed. But then that, I suppose, is the nature of all such books that try to capture images and memories of the past. The photographs that are included are always selective: first by the constraints and limitations of the photographer, then by the editor or publisher. But I always wondered what was round that next corner.

All my life I have been fascinated by the dual attraction of the past and the future – history and the world of tomorrow. Perhaps this apparent contradiction has enabled me to understand that, while we can only understand the present by better comprehending the past, at the same time all things must change and we are powerless to stop or reverse this inevitability. At the time, in my own naïve, haphazard way, I was just trying to record at least some of the old, or more interesting buildings, while already aware that so many were destined to disappear with each passing year.

The process of organised destruction of our heritage and past (done, of course, in the name of 'progress' or – more often – simple greed), which began in earnest in the 1960s, speeded up throughout the 1970s and into the 1980s, only to slow – although, of course, not actually stop – in the last fifteen years. Historians, architectural historians and conservationists might deplore the loss, but it still has to be said that as much bath water was thrown out with the occasional baby. Many of the buildings (including some pictured here) were neither attractive nor particularly functional; the only regret being that what replaced them was often even uglier and ultimately just as impractical.

Again, looking back at some of these pictures of 1970s Teddington, Twickenham and Hampton it is possible still to glimpse something of the village and small semi-rural towns these places once were – even within the lifetime of my parents, certainly my grandparents. Going back now, twenty or thirty years later, I see the inevitable triumph of suburbia; the housing estates, the blocks of flats or offices; the 'business parks' and industrial estates; the fast-food outlets, the wine bars that were once small shops, post offices or banks; the little community shops that are now – at best – boutiques or estate agents, or converted into houses; the high streets that all look alike. Thankfully, the wonderful rivers and parks, and the grand houses and palaces which continue to attract foreign tourists, *have* managed to survive.

Teddington, Twickenham and the Hamptons are now part of Greater London, the suburbs of which have since swept onward, to swallow up other small towns in Middlesex, Essex, Kent and Surrey. Historic Middlesex, the county I was born in, and lived half my life in, was wiped off the map at the stroke of a busy bureaucrat's pen – surviving only as a cricket club or the name of a hospital. Once the boundary between Middlesex and Surrey was the River Thames, but now, from the postal aspect Hampton Court is in Surrey.

L.P. Hartley once said that 'The past is another country', and it is only when we look at old photographs that we can appreciate just how much has changed – sometimes subtly, sometimes dramatically. What often only seems like the day before yesterday is itself now history, but – unlike the previous excellent books of Victorian and Edwardian Teddington, Twickenham and Hampton from the archives of the Borough of Twickenham Local History Society – mine is a recent history that many of us will still recollect.

For the most part the photographs speak for themselves, except where I have recorded some titbits of the past, dates or demolitions; otherwise I have relied on the local historians to fill or refresh the gaps in my knowledge or memory. My personal recollections and commentary, however, remain exclusively my own.

Teddington Lock from Ferry Road at high tide, mid-1970s.

1
TEDDINGTON

Those of my parents' generation still rue the day when the Borough of Twickenham took over the governance of Teddington. No good came of it, they said, and, when Richmond in turn swallowed up Twickenham, things could only get worse.

For most people not from Teddington or our part of Middlesex, my home town probably has only two significant reasons to remember it – the National Physical Laboratory, or NPL, as we always called it, one of the leading centres for scientific research in the UK; and Teddington Lock, the 'last lock on the Thames' (although there *is* another small lock and weir at Richmond, just below Twickenham Bridge), and the furthest tidal point – indeed, many old locals like to think Teddington means 'Tide's-end-town'.

For me, the alternative explanation of the name – that it probably derived from 'tun' of Tudda's people – is just as romantic and appealing, implying that Teddington had its origins in Anglo-Saxon times. That there is apparently no entry for Teddington in the Domesday Book is not, in itself, significant. It *is* mentioned in documents a few years later, in 1100. Middlesex itself is the territory of the 'Middle Saxons', and the dormant Anglo-Saxon in me (inherited perhaps from my eccentric grandfather Groombridge) finds some pleasure in the idea that a settlement at what is now Teddington is Anglo-Saxon rather than Anglo-Norman.

To my knowledge there are no Roman remains there, even though the Bath Road from Brentford to Staines ran further north, through what is now Hounslow. The first weir on the Thames at Teddington dates from the fourteenth century; and a lock was only built early in the nineteenth century. Going by old maps, in the days before the coming of the railway it remained a largely linear village – a cluster of houses, churches and shops along the old High Street, later spilling into what became Broad Street, surrounded by farmland, heath and common land.

Fleeting glimpses of that village atmosphere could still be seen occasionally in the 1970s; but today very little remains. Manor Road, next to Teddington Lock, now looks like Canary Wharf. Bland office buildings and box-like shop units now occupy the Broad Street/Waldegrave Road Bridge; everywhere the small community shops – greengrocers, newsagents and tobacconists, ironmongers, butchers and dairies – have vanished, often the physical structure of the shop itself has gone, while the entire area from Somerset Road to Walpole Road has been transformed, with old streets disappearing and what were once quiet little cul-de-sacs becoming through-roads, clogged with motor cars.

Teddington Lock viewed from the end of Ferry Road at high tide, 1970s. Even in the 1970s the frequent high tide often came sufficiently far up Ferry Road to make access to the suspension bridge almost impossible for those pedestrians without wellington boots. The area had not yet completely succumbed to the late twentieth-century obsession with making everything neat and tidy, organised and orderly, at the expense of character.

The metal walkway has gone, and has been replaced by a rather ugly, but solid brick wall that incorporates a stepped seated area. Now, however, on the old suspension bridge there are ramps, catwalks, barbed-wire fences and barricades. In the 1960s and '70s this area still retained a comparatively rural atmosphere; no one seemed in a great hurry as working barges and small pleasure-cruisers still came through the lock. Walking back across Ham Meadows late at night (as I often did in my teens and early twenties) was neither intimidating nor frightening; while the Surrey towpath was often muddy and flooded, negotiable by only the most determined walker.

Ferry Road from Lock Island, 1970s. The old Victorian boathouse and the rear of big houses on Manor Road are on the opposite bank. The suspension bridge is on the left just out of the picture. From 1934 onwards the boathouse belonged to the British Motor Yacht Club.

Unfortunately, a combination of man-made and natural obstructions prevented me duplicating the previous view from exactly the same angle. A metal gantry and locked gate now jut out from the island; ramps for disabled wheelchair-users spiral around the bridge steps; new steps lead down to the sandy beach; while, from the footpath that runs along the island towards the Lock, trees and foliage screen a clear glimpse of the Teddington bank. The boathouse is still there, but the big, elegant riverside houses have all been swept away, replaced by a massive new residential complex, known as Quay West.

The Old Vicarage from Kingston Road, facing the Lensbury Club Sports Ground, with the roof of St Alban's Church behind and Udney Hall Gardens out of the picture to the left. St Alban's Church, the so-called 'Cathedral of South Middlesex', built and consecrated between 1885 and 1889, became a local landmark, its green copper roof visible for miles around, most notably from the top of Richmond Hill.

The Old Vicarage, now 2 Kingston Road, has been divided into flats, 2006. The trees and fence have gone, and there are dormer windows in the roof. Like the great, grandiose St Alban's Church itself (which ceased to be a church in 1967 and is now the Landmark Arts Centre), the vicarage building has survived.

Ferry Road into Teddington High Street and 'Peg Woffington Cottages', 163–7 High Street, viewed from Langham Road. The cottages date from 1759. It is not known whether the eighteenth-century Irish actress Peg Woffington ever lived in one of the cottages. She died in 1760 and is buried in St Mary's Church.

In 2006 the tall trees behind the cottages have gone and the small open space on the corner of a now truncated Twickenham Road has been tidied up. Thankfully, Peg Woffington Cottages are comparatively unchanged – even the hedge is still there. However, the small workingman's end-terrace cottage (a later addition, built in about 1850) has lost its chimney but gained completely inappropriate replacement windows.

Nos 155–3 Eton Villas of 1864 (although, despite the date on the wall, they were not occupied until 1868); and nos 151–49 Harrow Villas. According to research carried out some years ago by P.A. Ching, between the late 1860s and the '90s they were mostly occupied by professional men (solicitors, surgeons and so on) and their families; most of whom were incomers to the Teddington area. However, by the 1890s it would appear they were mainly tenanted by various lodgers and boarders, and between 1902 and 1912 Harrow Villas was a girls' school, and Eton Villas a school of music.

I think these grand (but rather typical) houses not only symbolise both a lost architectural style and way of life, but also give a good indication of just how delightfully (and unashamedly) middle class and bourgeois this whole area once was. By the 1970s and 1980s they were occupied by students from St Mary's College, but by the 1990s they had again become private residences. Unfortunately, the wonderful cedar of Lebanon, visible in the old photograph above, has gone.

Nos 119–23 High Street, between Watts Lane and Cambridge Road, 1970s. According to the local historians, nos 119 and 119A are one of two surviving houses out of five that originally stood between the King's Head and Watts Lane. They were built early in the eighteenth century, only being converted into commercial shop units in the 1920s.

No. 119 is Maude, removals, transport and storage, which was still in business as late as 1999. No. 119A was Daytronics, a television, electrical and hi-fi store; next to which was no. 121 (listed in a trade directory as HGF Fruit and Vegetable Shop, which had already gone by 1981). By 1999 this was Handy Hardware. Beyond this, in the distance, can be seen the King's Head public house, commemorating Charles I and dating originally from the seventeenth century, although extensively renovated and restyled since then. The present buildings date from the nineteenth century.

Today the front forecourt of the King's Head is walled and, although still retaining its old name, is named the l'Auberge Restaurant, which used to be at the foot of Hill Rise, Richmond. No. 119 is now Di Olivo Delicatessen, while 119A is Teddington Hardware; beyond that, next to the King's Head, no. 121 is Nichols, a goldsmith. A modern pedestrian bridge extends over the side-road, which leads to Marks & Spencer's customer car park.

Nos 103–7 High Street, H.H. Howell, next to no. 107, a fashion and hosiery shop, which in 1971 was Mary Coe, Lingerie & Costume Wear. Immediately next door, and within the same delightful parade of shops and yards, were 99–101 High Street, F.M.E. Stroud, grocer. Next to Stroud's the gateway of no. 97A, then possibly still G. and W. Cars, later St Albans Car Sales. Both Howell and Stroud had already changed by 1981. Although there was an older building on this site dating back to the seventeenth century, this building was constructed in 1840, with the shops being built on the front sometime between 1900 and 1908.

This entire block of shops has been demolished and replaced by a Marks & Spencer food store. Although the new frontage is low and in keeping with the rest of the High Street, one cannot help but lament the loss of the original shops, which had such character and individuality.

Nos 91–7 High Street, with the corner of Watts Lane on the left, 1970. No. 91 was then Bernard Miles, optician (probably rebuilt during the nineteenth century); while nos 93–5 were Brookers Hardware Stores from 1928 to 1991. Parts of the red-roofed no. 93 may date back to the sixteenth century. The inscriptions on the upper-storey façade are advertising Crown, Dulux and Magicote paints. By 1999 it had already become Mobile World. According to the 1971 to 1975 directories, no. 97 was F.P. Burtenshaw, fishmonger.

The same stretch of Teddington High Street in 2006. No. 97, seen in both photographs, once located next to the white gateway to the motor car repairs, is now Ted's Children's Clothes, catering for ages nought to sixteen years; no. 95 – which had been part of Brookers until it ceased trading – later underwent restoration and is now the Tanning Centre. No. 93 has become Net. Com. The delightful old hardware shop, with its multitude of produce hanging up outside under the striped awning, has given way to what is perhaps very much the more typical 'shop of our time' – selling mobile phone accessories. No. 91 is now a small bistro.

No. 87 High Street, 1970s. A. Geere, a cycle shop, had a lean-to glass extension, and part of the canopy and façade of Stapleton & Sons, butcher, visible on the left. The cottages behind Geere's shop are thought to date back to the sixteenth century. Geere's had ceased trading by 1981.

The lean-to and the old shop front have gone, while the new façade, with its shrunken upstairs windows, is typically bland and without any character. It is now Studio M – Prints, Period Lighting, Porcelain. On the right, no. 89 is now Teddington Post Office, which replaced the original larger, grander, but more functional building further up the High Street, just down from the distinctive Lloyds Bank building.

Nos 83–5 High Street, 1970s. From the 1950s until 1980 these premises were Stapleton & Sons, butchers. There was a shop and house on this site in 1800, but the larger frontage dates from 1863, when it was already a butcher's shop. The old original building still had wattle and daub walls when it was renovated in the 1980s. In the colour original the building is white and the striped canopy is red and white.

Since the 1980s Stapleton & Sons has been Shambles Wine Bar, and outwardly is comparatively unchanged; even the delightful old wooden cover-way or canopy over the pavement has survived.

Nos 79–81 High Street, March 1971. The main building (described in 1800 as being 'two freehold houses') dates from the eighteenth century and was possibly built in about 1790. The shop, no. 81, was at the time of this photograph Joan Jarman's antique shop. On my original slide I noted that it had previously been a pharmacy, and this was confirmed by Luke Denison at the Local Studies Library, who found it listed in the 1940 *Kelly's Directory* as P. Stacey & Son, chemist. No. 79 was Ken's barber's shop. The shop façades were probably built on the front of the older property in about 1891.

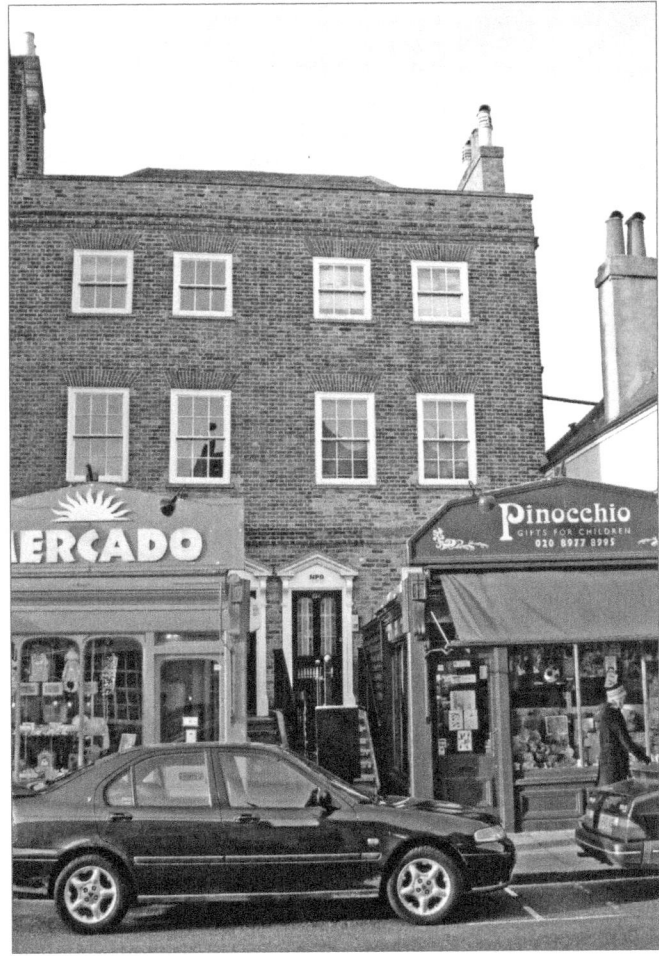

Repainted, with the (old and delightful) front shop-sign altered and the old façade of no. 81 appropriately modernised, this is now Pinocchio, while the adjacent former hairdresser, although in 1999 also Pinocchio, is now renamed Mercado. The lovely eighteenth-century houses behind are relatively untouched although the front doors have been repainted.

Nos 77–3 High Street and Wades Lane, seen from Field Lane, 1970s. No. 77 was W. Langrish & Sons, shoe shop, which survived into the 1990s until being devastated by a gas cylinder fire in 1992. In 1973 the unidentified middle shop, no. 75, which I originally thought from my photograph might have been a launderette, was Charles Dobnet, greengrocer; while no. 73, on the corner of Wades Lane, was the antique shop Collector's Corner, and later – in the 1990s – was Jeeves Interiors.

Again, from very early in the nineteenth century three cottages originally occupied this site, but they were demolished sometime in the second half of the century for the existing three-storey shops. Wades Lane was first recorded in 1871.

No. 73 is currently Jude the Obscure, a clothes shop, while no. 75 is now L'Amandine, a French patisserie, and no. 77 has become Antiques Doors & Brass. It is still just possible to see the faint outline on the brick side-wall facing Wades Lane, where the billboard posters once were. One subtle improvement between the past and present pictures is the disappearance or reduction of unsightly television aerials – particularly noticeable here.

The Kings Arms public house, High Street and Wades Lane, from Field Lane, 1970. Local historian P.A. Ching tells me that these were originally three cottages with yards and outbuildings, again probably dating from the early nineteenth century. Another three cottages from the same period once stood on the other side of Wades Lane, where nos 77–3 now stand, and four more to the west, while other small houses and buildings were located behind, accessed even then by what later became Wades Lane.

The Kings Arms – originally occupying just the corner cottage on what became Wades Lane – was certainly licensed as a beer-house by at least 1871, perhaps even earlier. The middle cottage was probably incorporated into the public house in about 1891.

New bollards, chimneys lopped off, the upper balustrade gone, a façade makeover, and the name of the old brewery gone (as has, thankfully, the concrete street-light); the adjacent surviving cottage with its picket fence, has now also been incorporated into the public house itself, with bench seats outside. Unfortunately, however, much of the previous rural character and cosiness of the old pub have been lost in the process.

No. 67 and part of 65 High Street, in about March 1971. In 1973 the building was listed as being Caffyne and Brown, Warehouse. No. 65 was the Winter Proof Heating Co. Originally four cottages, dating from at least 1829 on this site, with a passageway between nos 61–3 and 65–7, they may have been renovated or rebuilt in the mid-nineteenth century. Throughout much of the first half of the twentieth century no. 65 was occupied by Langrish Boot Repairs, which later moved to no. 77. All four shops were demolished between 1972 and 1981.

The site was occupied by an Ottakar's bookshop in 2006 but is now a Waterstone's. The original front door of the cottage adjacent to the King's Arms can be seen in both photographs. Although the passageway has been retained in the new design, the character of the old Victorian cottages and shop fronts has been sadly lost. Between 1989 and 1993 the new shop unit was occupied by Sofa Bed City.

No. 61 and part of 63 High Street, in about March 1971. Listed in trade directories as Caffyne & Brown, no. 61 was a printer, which burnt down in 1972, after which no. 63 was allowed to fall into disrepair. The whole block was demolished sometime between 1972 and 1981. No. 63 was the Delicatessen Deli.

Again it is interesting to compare the roofline, chimneys, upstairs windows and the shop fronts of this parade of four shops; each was different, although nos 61 and 67 were obviously under the same ownership. The number boarding is orange, the doors and lower façade dark olive green.

All of the above had already changed or disappeared by 1981. In 2006 it is the site of Mum and Me, which specialises in fancy-dress. The old brown brickwork has been replaced by an undistinguished yellow box.

Nos 55–1 High Street, March 1971. No. 55 was BRZ Ltd, a 'warehouse'; no. 53 E. & R. Kirby, and no. 51 the Charcoal Grill restaurant.

No. 53 is still E. & R. Kirby's Pharmacy in 2006, although the original shop façade has unfortunately been modernised. The adjacent no. 55 is now the Teddington Bookshop. These shops were built on what had once been, long ago, the front gardens of grand houses facing the old High Street. The upper floors and interesting roofline of the original old houses are visible behind them, and are still comparatively unchanged.

Nos 47 to 51 High Street, viewed from Cedar Road, and unfortunately taken with the basic Kodak box camera on a dark winter's day, early in the 1970s. These were the shops built on the frontage of St Mary's Vicarage, which originally dated from 1837.

No. 47, which had previously been John Lay, then the A. Bedric Barrett Liquormart, grocer and off-licence, in 1972, and in 1994 Freddie Barrett's Wine Shop, is still an off-licence – now part of the Threshers chain. What had been Frederic of Kensington, hair stylist, at no. 49, is now the Hair Studio; while no. 51 is now Wok This Way. The tree on the corner of Cedar Road in the foreground of the 1971 photograph has gone, but a new tree has been planted between nos 47 and 49, certainly an improvement.

Bridge Approach, High Street into Broad Street, 1970s. Even in the 1970s this still looked much the same as in old photographs from the early twentieth century, with its parade of shops leading down towards Park Road on the left, while extending towards Broad Street, with Barclays Bank in the distance on the right. On its prominent corner, facing the bridge itself, was Teddington Model Supplies, 86 Broad Street, which I remember, as a young boy in the 1950s, as a fascinating treasure-trove of a place. Next door, 2–4 Park Road, is Subway 4, with a Pepsi advertisement, presumably a café. Vacant in 1971, in the 1975 trade directory is it listed as the Upstairs Downstairs Restaurant & Snack Bar. Again in 1975, no. 6 was A.W. Strokes & Sons, Builders; no. 8 was Bissell & Birch, apparently a workshop; no. 10 was Campion Products; and the parade ended at no. 12, Moss & Co., solicitors.

In 2006 the former Park Road shops on the left, nearest The Causeway, have been demolished and replaced by the usual brick office-over-shops-style buildings; while no. 86 is, or was until recently, the Glossary, an independent greetings card shop. Although the shops have all changed names, and the long, double-frontage of Sneller's estate agency is rather intrusive, the appearance is much the same – even the clock. The most obvious other changes are to the street furniture – new pedestrian barrier, street-lighting and traffic islands. Unfortunately the rest of the bridge has been transformed: the Waldegrave Road shops have been demolished and replaced, and the area between the bridge and the railway station has been redeveloped.

St Mary and St Peter's Infant and Junior Public School, or Church of England School, originally located on the corner of Broad Street and Church Road. Built in about 1868, it was demolished in 1979 together with the Grade II listed St Peter and St Paul Church opposite, despite local protest – effectively taking away a key part of Teddington's historical heart. The new school was built further down Church Road, obliterating Argyle Road in the process, as well as the few houses and shops in the two roads that had survived the bombing in the Second World War.

The new church in 2006, looking nothing like a church should; more like a hybrid between a fire-station and an underground bunker, and with an ugly metal fence. It occupies much of what had been the site of the old junior school, in what is now styled Bychurch End. The ancient tree that once dominated the walled playground (it can just be glimpsed in the older picture) is still there, now incorporated into a small enclosed garden, accessible from the bridge. However, only about a third of the old outer school wall has survived. Much of the soft red brick wall, carved with the initials, names and graffiti of generations of Teddington children, has – like the school itself – gone forever.

Public Library, Waldegrave Road, 1970s. It was just down from the Paint Research Association building, with its flat roof and paint testing panels. The stone plaque over the entrance reads 'Carnegie Library 1905'. The old no. 27 bus, from its terminus at Teddington station, in Adelaide Road, stopped immediately outside, going to Twickenham, Richmond, Sheen and eventually Archway, north London.

In 2006 the exterior is almost completely unchanged, but on a recent visit I was amazed at how the library interior too was much as I remembered it in the 1960s and '70s. Apart from the central desk area, which was then quite elaborate, the individual rooms still seemed to be the same, and served the same functions – reference room, reading room, children's section – while the walls of the main library were still panelled in dark wood, and the French windows still opened out onto the secluded walled garden at the back. The bus stop now has a modern shelter and the façade has been freshly cleaned. The building seen to the right of the earlier photograph has gone.

Church Lane, off Church Road, 1970s. This wonderful example of old working-class backstreet cottages, stables and yards was sadly demolished not long after this photograph was taken, in 1972. Former Teddington resident Graham Barrett confirmed that the building on the right was once the local smithy; while the end buildings were probably the yard used by an elderly 'rag and bone' man, who, even I can remember in my childhood during the 1950s, used to ride around on a cart and horse (like Steptoe & Son) calling out a plaintive, 'Ra'bone, ra'bone . . .'

The site is now occupied by 7, 5 and 3 Church Lane; a terrace of modern town-houses, which could be anywhere. With its ubiquitous line of parked cars, this once fascinating little side-street, backing onto the railway, now has virtually no atmosphere.

Nos 44–34 Church Road, Sidney Villas, just down from Sydney Road. Many were still shops up until the late 1950s.

Today the old shop façades are less obvious and all have been converted into houses – the fate sadly shared by so many small shops throughout the country since the dominance of the supermarket. Most have modern replacement mock-nineteenth-century square-paned lower-floor windows that do not sit well with the older sash windows on the upper floor. Note also the nose-to-tail parked cars.

No. 1 Bridgeman Road, from Station Road, 1970s. This building was originally associated with nearby Christ Church (an Anglican Free Church), and may even have been the vicarage. The building at the side, facing Station Road, was apparently numbered 11 Station Road.

Today the building is 1 Churcham House. It is still recognisable, although the original red brickwork has now been plastered and colour-washed. The windows of the left-hand wing have been altered from their original, indicating a possible change in floor levels, while the central tower has had another floor added together with a pitched roof. The premises are now used by a number of companies. Unfortunately, I was unable to discover any definite or detailed previous history of this property.

H. Comfort & Son, coal merchant, Fuel Order Office, Station Road, just down from Teddington railway station, probably built in the 1870s or 1880s and a reminder not only of when almost every railway station had its own goods yard but also, perhaps, how – even into the 1970s – many houses were still reliant on coal fires for heating. The notice in the gateway reads 'NO CARS ALLOWED IN YARD PLEASE'. In the background, across the old station yard, can be seen A.K. Motors Ltd. I was reminded that a similar building (also a coal office) once stood on the bridge itself, where Informer House now is, belonging to Charrington's Fuel Office, but unfortunately it has since been demolished.

Today 42 Station Road is the Teddington Cheese, and incorporated into Teddington Business Park. Although this is a protected building, much of the station yard is now Enterprise Way, comprising a nursery garden next to the station itself; the usual bland, box-like, windowless industrial units; the huge intrusive office block which was originally a training centre for Barclays Bank (now named Park House); and – incorporated into the bridge itself – Informer House, collectively creating a dusty, unattractive urban desert.

Victoria Road and Adelaide Road, 1970s. Here Victoria Road and Adelaide Road are amalgamated into what almost seemed like a small square – then still comparatively free of cars – with R. & E. Martin's, another cosy little shop, located immediately opposite the main building of the mid-nineteenth-century railway station: ideally situated for commuters, who could buy the morning paper and a snack before catching the train or bus. When I lived in Bolton Gardens I often walked over the footbridge from Station Road and along the wonderfully atmospheric Railway Passage, emerging into this little 'square' next to the Railway Hotel. The no. 27 bus, which later become the no. 37, terminated here, next to The Cedars.

Although buses now run down nearby Park Road, the convenience of a bus–rail interchange has gone, while, typically, as the rail yard was redeveloped no thought was given to commuter car-parking facilities. The quiet square is now one hideous, disorganised car park, minus even the convenience of a newsagent, which has suffered the usual fate of the corner-shop, having been part-converted into a bland, nondescript house. Although what survived was, I believe, still a newsagent/confectioner's until recently, it is now the Personal Training Centre. There is now a small news stall in the booking-hall of the railway station, a rather inferior substitute.

Nos 31–3 Park Road and the corner of Adelaide Road, 1970s. These shops went through a number of metamorphoses; the small shop unit was a newsagent or confectioner at one time during this period.

No. 31 is now Spivack, a chemist, while the smaller no. 33 is Moonstone, jeweller, designer and valuer. On the corner, Hughenden House is now the Park Road Dental Centre. Several of the trees in the grounds of The Cedars (the 1950s-built housing estate, accessible from Adelaide Road) have disappeared. Again the overall effect is more urban and less rural.

The Coach House, 20A Park Road, probably nineteenth century, 1970s. The coach house is all that is left of a house known as St Mary's, no. 20, which was demolished after the Second World War. The old, brown brick wall, with its ancient shady avenue of trees, originally extended towards Park Lane and once enclosed Teddington Lodge (formerly no. 18). It is now the site of the modern 1960s police station which replaced the old Teddington police station in Church Road.

The trees are still there in 2006, together with bits of the wall. The shabby old wooden seat has been replaced by a sculptural metal one; the period cars by contemporary models. The lovely old tree in the Coach House yard has gone.

No. 106 Park Road, Park House, viewed from the Park Road/Queen's Road junction, 1970s. Although there are references to an earlier structure as long ago as the seventeenth century, the present building probably dates from the late eighteenth and was certainly called Park House in 1872. Between 1900 and the 1920s the surrounding land (which had totalled 6 acres) was sold and systematically built on. From the 1930s it was a nursing home for aged ladies, and the name was changed to Frithville.

Now Park Lodge, 149 Queen's Road and Park House. It was sold in the 1980s and subsequently divided into three. The old three-storey house reverted to its former name, while the adjoining two-storey building became Park Lodge. Although both buildings are still comparatively unchanged, somehow the stately rural atmosphere of the early photograph is now gone, even the angle was difficult to replicate in 2006. The old brick wall in front of Park House has been heightened with a lighter mismatch brick. There is now a constant stream of traffic emerging from Queen's Road, new traffic islands at the junction with Park Road and a huge new housing development opposite, on the ground that was once part of the ARL (Admiralty Research Laboratory) before it moved to Haslar and Portland, and the Crown Estate sold the land.

Nos 10 and 8 Hampton Road, Edwardian houses opposite Coleshill Road. They are just down from where the old pre-war Wesleyan chapel once stood. According to P.A. Ching these houses were built sometime in the 1880s or 1890s, and were once the Huntington House private school. Two more houses from that same period used to stand in Stanley Road, where the postwar church now is, but they were destroyed during the Second World War.

Unfortunately, the delightful roofline of nos 10 and 8 has changed; and the attractive and distinctive corner turrets – which had dormer-windows and matched the slightly elevated, lighter brickwork of the grand entrance-porches at each end – have gone.

Another view of nos 8–10, with 12–14 Hampton Road, and no. 16 beyond that, 1970. Besides the omnipresent concrete lamp-post there existed a mismatch of rather ugly, low brick walls, wooden and wire fences and gates fronting the road. Only the old red-brick gateway (centre) was probably original.

A tree and bushes now separate no. 10 from 12, somewhat obstructing the old façade, but otherwise (unlike its near neighbour) this second semi-detached house appears to have survived the years comparatively unchanged or mutilated. No. 16, Shrewsbury House, seen in the distance, is now painted white and is home to Scots Group Insurance. The young trees in the previous picture never reached maturity, while a new functional bus-shelter is now outside the low, single-storey, red-brick Teddington Methodist Sunday School building, itself almost opposite the old Cottage Hospital. The street-light and fences have gone, and there is an attractive open-plan front garden.

This delightful red-brick house in Hampton Road, photographed in December 1970, already looked sadly derelict; it has since been demolished. It dated from the 1880s or '90s. This was a fate shared by several other large houses situated to the left, between here and Gloucester Road.

Detective work eventually revealed that Oakhurst Close now stands on this site. The fir tree in the background and the distinctive side and roofline of 24 Hampton Road, Cambridge House, can just be seen on the right-hand side of the 1970s photograph. The new development, while functional, is not very interesting. Cambridge House, probably also built in the 1890s, was once the Oakton Nursing Home.

Fairholm House, a former hotel, at 42 Hampton Road, on the corner of Anlaby Road, December 1970. In 1937 it was owned by Mrs L. Blackwell and, according to my mother, owned by Mr Wright and Joy Miles in the late 1940s, then still a hotel. Fairholm was one of three Victorian houses: the adjacent nos 40–38 were the offices of the National Life and General Assurance Co. Ltd, even in the 1930s. They are all believed to date from before 1865. I have some personal affiliation with this building, as it was here, sometime in 1946–7, that my parents first met; my father was staying at the hotel with his mother, and my mother was working in the garden.

According to newspaper reports at the time, it was against some considerable local opposition that all three houses, nos 42–38, were scheduled for demolition sometime between 1975 and 1979 for the construction of National Life Insurance's new three-storey office block, although it would seem that certainly no. 38 (and possibly even part of no. 40) was eventually reprieved and incorporated into the new building. When National Life went into receivership it was taken over by Haymarket Publishing, which moved from their premises in London's Regent Street in May 1979; work on the site finished early in 1980. What had been Fairholm itself is now the site of a sunken landscaped garden. Haymarket Publishing moved out in 2005.

Waldegrave Road, viewed from Shacklegate Lane, 1970s. The shops seen here are, from left to right, no. 158, A. Smith, tailor; no. 156, A.E. Lynch & Sons, grocers (both apparently dating back to at least 1940, appearing in the last *Kelly's Directory* for that area); no. 154, Biddy (the nature of whose business I have been unable to discover . . . perhaps a boutique or fashion shop? In 1940 it was a sweet shop); and finally (with the awning), no. 152, R.G. Millers & Sons, butchers.

A traffic island is now situated in the middle of Shacklegate Lane. No. 158 has become Candlelight Antiques; no. 156 is Jo McLaren Evening Wear; no. 154 is at present an empty shop; while no. 152 is still Millers, which has been there for over forty years. No. 150 (not visible in the earlier photograph) ends the parade, and is a grocer's and off-licence/newsagent's. No. 209, the Waldegrave Arms public house, is on the right, although in late 2006 it was closed amid rumours of redevelopment.

The Old Stables, 125 Strawberry Vale, viewed from Waldegrave Park, 1970s. Apart from the assumption that they once *were* stables, the only other information discovered is that the 1953 telephone directory lists the occupant as one 'H. Hampton (Lord)'.

Opposite, below, and this page: Apart from road markings and new street-lighting, the scene is basically unchanged. Even the tree is still recognisable on the corner of Waldegrave Park. However, closer inspection of the second photograph reveals the alteration. The metal gates have gone and the Old Stables are now urban residential rather than rural.

Radnor Works, between nos 51 and 71; Strawberry Vale, demolished in 1972. According trade directories in 1937, this was the head office of Arthur L. Gibson & Co., Manufacturing Engineers (with branch offices in Glasgow, Manchester and Birmingham), which made and patented the 'Kinnear Steel Rolling Shutter'. Fifteen years later, the site was occupied by J.B. Marr & Co. Ltd, Electrical Engineers. The directories also refer to an adjacent Beacon Lodge, presumably residential.

The site has changed out of all recognition. Mallard Place, an extensive residential development with planted and well-established trees, paved cul-de-sac, elegant houses and apartments has replaced the industrial premises. According to newspaper articles from the period the history of the proposed redevelopment of this 4½-acre site, listed as being between 53 and 95 Strawberry Vale, was extremely controversial and contentious. The arguments raged from 1973 to 1978, but it would perhaps appear that the objections were as much politically motivated as by any concern for the environment or local residents. In 1975, after the first proposal for flats and houses was rejected following one inquiry, Labour-controlled Wandsworth Borough Council put in an application to build between 120 and 125 council flats on the site, against the wishes of a then Conservative Richmond Borough Council, as well as the local residents. Finally, another three years later, in 1978 the original property company got the go-ahead to build a revised redevelopment, with public access to the riverfront.

Above and overleaf: The huge Stoney Deep house, 48 Twickenham Road, demolished 1976, viewed in a series of photographs from Grove Gardens, opposite, 1970s. As with Radnor Works, this redevelopment proved somewhat contentious, the original application being made in 1972. After this was refused in 1973 (ironically for today's Twickenham Road, the Council objection was that the development would be of 'excessive density and out of scale with the riverside area'), a new plan was submitted the following year, and final approval was given in 1976. Built in the 1890s and first occupied by a Mr Beal, a seed merchant, the house was later a nurses' home.

Again, nothing remains to link the old photographs with the view today. Although still named Stoney Deep, it is now a cul-de-sac of attractive two- and three-storey apartments, landscaped gardens, trees and views across the river. Local campaigners won right of way access along the riverside in 1989.

Broom Road, June 1970. To judge from the barbed-wire fence in the foreground this photograph was probably taken during, or not long after, the construction of this block of flats.

Now Hamble Court, 1 Broom Park, part of a complex cul-de-sac of housing located at the top of Normansfield Avenue, where Broom Road becomes the Lower Teddington Road. Once almost exclusively given over to early twentieth-century Edwardian and 1920s and '30s middle-class houses that typified what used to be called the 'leafy suburbs', in the last thirty years extensive new developments have sprung up, especially along the river, and are now being constructed in the grounds of the old Normansfield Hospital itself.

No. 33 Cromwell Road, situated on the corner of Udney Park Road and viewed from Fairfax Road, 1970s. I have been unsuccessful in my attempts to discover the identity or history of this elegant red-brick house, but we can assume that it was probably contemporary with Redlands, opposite. I recollect that, even in the 1970s, a part of Udney Park Road between Cornwall Road and the High Street was still gravelled and unsurfaced.

The same view today sees only the rear wall and house façades of 4–3 Davenport Close, the new development, the entrance of which opens out into Udney Park Road. The delightful Edwardian semi-rural atmosphere; the tall, well-established trees; the glimpse of open space beyond – all this has gone. The two smaller trees on the Cromwell Road pavement have survived but not much else. Looking at detailed Ordnance Survey maps from the early 1970s, it is possible to see how gradually the big houses, with their large gardens and empty adjacent lands, in Udney Park Road, Cromwell Road and the top end of Fairfax Road, succumbed to the bulldozer, and blocks of flats were built in their place.

Redlands in 1977, on the corner of Cromwell Road and Fairfax Road, another big red-brick, late Victorian house, probably contemporary with the house opposite. The street sign for Fairfax Road can just be glimpsed on the right, and the name (and number – 154) was on the brick gateposts.

Demolished sometime between 1971 and 1977, Redlands was replaced by another block of flats, thankfully half-hidden by trees, with the new entrance located further along Cromwell Road, just beyond Udney Park Road.

Nos 13–15 Blackmores Grove, 1970s. Much of Blackmores Grove is the usual, rather mixed suburban housing, Edwardian houses, small flats and council houses. This little terrace at the Bridgeman Road end constitutes the original, older cottages.

For many years no 11 (glimpsed left) was the rented home of my indomitable great-aunt 'Lizzie', Mary Elizabeth Needs, née Cross (1879–1984), my maternal grandmother's eldest sister, who moved here not long after she married in 1905, and continued to live there for the next 74 years (the last thirty years as a widow) until just after she was aged 100, when she moved in with her daughter in Twickenham, eventually passing away aged 105. During that time there was no electricity, no bath and only an outside toilet!

Many of the street trees in both Teddington and Twickenham have survived. The simple nature of the original cottages has been modified, however. The mishmash of contrasting window styles and concrete driveways gradually replacing front gardens had already started in the 1970s, but now wooden gates and porches are being replaced, and new extensions built, with modern yellowy bricks.

2
TWICKENHAM

Of the three locations included in this book I lived in Twickenham for the shortest period, from 1977 to 1981, and I have few memories of and little attachment to the place. The best thing about Twickenham, at that time, was that it had several good bookshops, although Richmond was still my preference. Perhaps because I was already in my late twenties and early thirties I was more detached from Twickenham, which never had the same intimacy or associations as Teddington, Hampton Hill or Hanworth.

Like Teddington, Twickenham was already inhabited during the Anglo-Saxon period. Although the earliest documentary evidence of the existence of 'Tuican hom' or 'Tuiccanham' dates from AD 704, there was almost certainly a settlement long before that time, perhaps even in Neolithic times, and recent excavations in the Amyand Park Road area have unearthed Roman remains. The southern Middlesex plain was extremely fertile agricultural land, with farms, orchards and market gardens growing fruit and vegetables for the insatiable London market by the sixteenth or seventeenth century. Between the seventeenth and nineteenth centuries Twickenham became *the* fashionable place for the nobility, who built many grand houses along the river, and some can still be seen, although sadly not all, and very few still as private houses.

However, even in the 1970s suburban Twickenham still had tantalising glimpses of the small rural town it had once been. The George public house and restaurant in King Street still had the archway to what had once been the stables and yard of the coaching inn; Church Road had the cosy, old-fashioned seventeenth-century Fox public house, where you stepped down several feet from the modern street level; and in the late 1960s a delightful old-fashioned bookshop called Langton's of the sort that has now almost completely disappeared, a rambling shop of low doorways, steps to different levels, wooden staircases and a lean-to extension that looked out onto a paved, weed-filled backyard. Still Langton's, it was later modernised, and much of this ramshackle quality was lost. Just briefly and rarely, perhaps on wet and misty days, walking along Church Lane to the Embankment, it was possible to imagine stepping back a hundred or two hundred years and to visualise the tumbledown wooden cottages, boats dragged up on the muddy foreshore, sailing-craft instead of motor-boats, huddled figures making their way to church, cobbled filthy streets, back alleys and poky doorways leading to dark courtyards.

Bit by bit, however, what was left of this atmosphere has been steadily eroded, as new shops and buildings have replaced the old. Queens Road, Station Yard and Railway

Approach are now almost unrecognisable, while the area boxed between London Road, Amyand Park Road and Arragon Road has likewise been redeveloped. But most of the changes are piecemeal and gradual – the slow invasion of the high street chain-stores and fast-food restaurants; the disappearance of the old Odeon cinema on the corner of Cross Deep; development of the Embankment and waterfront; and, of course, the universal disappearance of small shops and businesses. To my surprise, a few long-established shops have survived and continue to flourish – for instance, Blay's Motorcycles, Chapman's on the corner of Colne Road, Maple Leaf Pharmacy on the Green, Cousin's the greengrocer's in King Street. And, along Heath Road especially, there are still many small individual shops and restaurants, rather than the names that have made every English high street look the same.

Nos 205–7 Hampton Road, Fulwell, between Grove Road and the Mall School, 1970s. At the time of the original photograph it appeared to be derelict and the lower floor boarded up.

When I went back to take this photograph I expected the house to have been demolished, but instead it was still there, renovated and concealed behind a high wall. I was puzzled just how I had been able to take the original photograph, especially from the direction and angle. Another interesting feature is that architecturally this is a mirror-image house – the front is the same as the back!

No. 130 Hampton Road, 1970s. This is one of several delightful early nineteenth-century properties between Fulwell and Twickenham, in this instance located between Fourth Cross and Trafalgar Roads. Built in about 1840, the house was formerly known as 3 Nelson Terrace.

Even when the photograph was enlarged, I was unable to read the house number, so this image was particularly difficult to identify because several of the neighbouring houses are quite similar in appearance and design. Only eventually did a letter from the current owner confirm it *was* definitely the same house, having been restored in the 1980s from the rather plain façade of my earlier photograph, to what he termed its 'former glory'. The result is very obviously a labour of love and a shining example to other renovators.

Nos 36–2 Hampton Road, shops and the Prince Albert public house between Second and First Cross Roads, 1970s. At this time all three shops were still serving the community – selling foodstuffs, groceries, confectionery and newspapers. No. 36 appeared under the name E.L. Smith, grocer, in a 1973 trade directory. No. 32 was T.A. Hardy, greengrocer, until 1975, when the property was sold for £12,000, being in a state of almost total dereliction, and a year later it became Centre 32, a day-care centre run by the Twickenham & District Mental Health Association.

Sadly only the newsagent has survived as a retail outlet, being the Meet & Deep, and the present owners told me that they have been there for twenty-two years. No. 36, with skylights installed in the roof, is now the Creative Copy Centre. No. 32 is still Centre 32, now run by Richmond Borough Mind; while the Prince Albert, immediately next door, has had a complete makeover. Bill Weisblatt, Vice-Chair of Richmond Borough Mind, says that all three shops were probably converted from Victorian cottages.

No. 69 Hampton Road, opposite First Cross Road, 1970s. Although I was unable to discover the history or date of this property, local historian Tony Beckles Willson believed that it had once belonged to a doctor.

Now no longer residential, it is a small business centre, the old stables or outhouse being the Study Zone. The old tree that gives the early photograph its charm, is no longer. The area around the building is now a car park.

No. 64 Staines Road/The Green, then Twickenham Galleries, on the corner of May Road, and Grove Café opposite, viewed from The Green, 1970s. May Road used to be known as Stirling's Road, after one Thomas Stirling, who in the early part of the nineteenth century owned what is now 64 The Green. Despite its shape and size The Green was never a village green in the traditional sense. It was in fact a fragment of Hounslow Heath that was enclosed in the early nineteenth century, and used partly as allotments for the nearby workhouse (certainly until the mid-nineteenth century, although the workhouse itself was demolished in 1845), and partly for the pursuit of 'sports and pastimes', notably cricket. At various times it was also referred to as Twickenham Common, or the Little Common.

No. 64, with its delightful early nineteenth-century side and rear, brick and wooden extensions still visible from May Road, is now nameless, but used as small workshops. The former Grove Café site has been rebuilt, the billboard has gone and the corner building, 58 The Green, is now Ask, an Italian restaurant.

The junction of Colne Road and Mereway Road, viewed from Mereway Road, 1970s. The working-class terrace houses are empty and boarded up, already waiting demolition. The surviving end-of-terrace shop, with its wooden gateway and curtains at the upstairs windows, is a Mecca bookmakers. Looming behind is the roof of the huge Automotive Engineering Works. The low, red-brick wall and railing on the left belongs to James Darby House, a home for the elderly.

The original view proved extremely elusive. Eventually Neal Chapman correctly located it, but, even with confirmation from Ralph Cox of the Twickenham Museum, it still took me several minutes to orientate myself to take the photograph reproduced here. The railing and wall of James Darby House are the only common features. Of the urban semi-industrial, working-class back-street, there is now almost no trace; although some small-scale industry, motor-repairs and other workshops and offices can still be found between Briar House (located about 100yd out of the picture to the right), and back along Mereway Road, again on the right, behind the original brown-brick wall. But where the terrace and huge engineering plant once was, is now Hunting Gate Mews.

No. 116 Colne Road, just along from the May Road junction, 1970s. According to Alec Wallace, the current occupant, this terrace of cottages was originally built for fruit farm labourers, and no. 120 (just out of the picture on the left), was the farmer's house. When his wife bought the property, over forty years ago, it had three gas lamps, no electricity, an outside toilet and only a cold-water tap.

Again it required real detective work to identify the site of the old photograph; something I only achieved when I revisited Twickenham to research this book. In 1976 a completely new side-extension was constructed, linking no. 116 with its neighbour. New street-lighting and a wood and glass porch complete the subtle alteration. It is perhaps still just possible to appreciate this area's fascinating history from the buildings that have survived; a mixture of workers' cottages, small Victorian villas, large eighteenth-century houses, the occasional farmhouse, pubs and inns (some of which were probably pretty disreputable in their time), light industry and even a brewery.

The coach house of Knowle House, 32 Colne Road, 1970s, immediately opposite the junction of Knowle Road, Albion Road and Colne Road. This is actually the old coach house at the side of the house itself. The servants' quarters were where the top window is on the left-hand side. Built in 1792 by Edward Chapman, Knowle House is still owned by the Chapman family, whose pet shop and mini garden centre (we used to refer to it as a 'corn chandler') is located where Colne Road joins Heath Road. It was named Knowle House in 1846 and during the middle and late nineteenth century it had a number of different occupants. In 1913 it was used as a furniture store. It was again occupied by Percy Chapman (Neal Chapman's father) in 1915.

Today the chimneys have gone, and the fencing on the wall has vanished, otherwise the building looks much the same. New townhouses have been built to the right.

The rear of Knowle House from Edwin Road, during demolition for redevelopment, late 1970s. The distinctive roof and back of the old coach house is on the left. The extensive development completely altered the character of the area. A number of older houses on the north side of Colne Road between the railway viaduct and Crane Road disappeared, as did the cluster of workshops, office suites and small industry along the south side of Edwin Road, opposite Warwick Road and Norcutt Road.

The rear of Knowle House from across a car park, with houses to the rear and along Colne Road to Marsh Farm Road, 2006.

Warwick Road from the upstairs bedroom window of no. 47, where I lived from 1977 to 1981. Built in about 1903, the terraced houses in Warwick Road and Hamilton Road had three bedrooms, living-room and front parlour, with kitchen, bathroom and toilet at the back. When we first moved there in 1977 many of the original working-class families were still living there, but gradually, as the older generation died off, young professional middle class moved in, slowly transforming both the community and the interior of the houses themselves.

Viewed from approximately the same direction, but from the pavement in front of no. 47, 2006. The façades of several of the houses have been renovated, and the street is now lined with parked cars. In 1977 a three-bedroom terraced house in Warwick Road cost about £10,000. By 1981 the price was already £30,000, and within another ten years was over £150,000 and still climbing. In spring 2006 the average price was anything from £275,000 to £325,000, and most owners have sacrificed the third bedroom for an upstairs bathroom.

The Old Coach House, Albion Road, sometime in the 1970s, viewed from the Collins Alley cut-way, which connects Albion Road to The Green. After the first edition had already gone to print I happened to meet a former resident who gave me some tantalising, but still interesting, snippets of Albion Road history. She believed that early in the twentieth century the Coach House was called 'Floral House', and had a connection to a public house that was once located to the right, which she thought went by the name of 'The British Flag'. I have not been able to confirm this (it is not in the 1899 Middlesex public house list under that name) but there was a 'PH" on that site on the 1894 OS map, with a cut-way to Colne Road beyond that. My informant understood the pub's main entrance was actually on Colne Road, then a well-used thoroughfare. Behind the Coach House may once have been a orchard, as there was a very old apple tree in the garden, which eventually died in the late 1990s. The property deeds also indicated that the property may have once been a shop, possibly a butchers. If nothing else, this example the often complex and confused history of this old part of Twickenham.

A new house (no. 15) on the corner of Albion Road and Collins Alley now blocks the view of the Old Coach House. The house on the right is just recognisable despite a new fence, windows and roof.

A fire-plaque indicates that the Old Coach House was quite old, perhaps late eighteenth or early nineteenth century. However, Neal Chapman maintains that, to his knowledge, it was never a coach house, so the name may just be more fanciful than functional. It stands in architectural isolation, and he recollects that the land to the left was once a bombsite.

The Green, and the junction of Hampton Road and Staines Road, with Knowle Road to the right; no. 20, Maple Leaf Pharmacy on the corner; and the old 1894 water pump, given by the Countess Waldegrave for use by the poor, visible in the foreground. The converging apex of the Staines and Hampton Roads may have once marked the gateway to the town. It is believed that the Pest House, or place of quarantine, was located nearby, though the exact site is unknown. The present pharmacist dated this photograph to sometime between 1972 and 1974, as it shows the new windows installed on the second floor.

In 2006 both the water pump and the Maple Leaf Pharmacy are still there. There has been a pharmacy on this site since 1880, when the existing building was constructed. The present owner has been there since 1965, and still has the original walnut wall-cabinets, several huge glass bottles inherited from the 1880 shop, now displayed in the window, and the old stove, now in the shop itself.

No. 18, on the corner of Knowle Road, in the 1970s, and in this photograph now Antiques & Modern Items, although in the picture on the opposite page, taken perhaps several years before, it was still a small patisserie or cake shop. Before that, until 1967 it was a newsagent's/confectionery shop.

Traffic lights now regulate the junction of Hampton Road and Staines Road, but otherwise Knowle Road is still one-way. The billboards on the wall of the shop have gone, and the middle cottage – no. 16 – has had new windows fitted and a front wall has replaced the old fence. No. 14 has lost its huge chimney, and no. 18 is still an antiques and junk shop.

The Green in the 1970s, with nos 10 and 8, the latter still being E. Moore, Bakers & Confectionery, whose reputation was such that customers were often known to queue out of the door and along the street. Next to that is no. 6, then Hygienic Applications Ltd, which, in the early 1950s, was once J.W Popplewell Stores; beyond that, what was once the old DER showroom, and which was later a carpet shop; and Scruby's Furniture. The further block is already empty, before being demolished in 1976–7. In the late 1960s DER had been a pioneer in television rental, the Head Office of which was the three-sided concrete-and-glass office block named Apex House, Hanworth, at the junction of Sunbury Way and Hampton Road West, next to the flyover of the M3 motorway, itself since demolished and now a car park. Apparently there was also a toy factory here, and at one time Fountain Luxury Coaches had its office at no. 12. Its coaches were parked in Knowle Road; new houses have been built on the original site.

Although no. 10 is still a cottage, recognisable by its windows, no. 12 is now an Indian restaurant, and no. 8 Jack the Stripper, door and furniture stripping. Nos 10 and 8 have new dormer windows in the roof.

Here The Green blends into Heath Road, with the then still white-fronted, two-storey building comprising no. 6, while the red-brick buildings (nos 4–2, which probably date from the early twentieth century) were later demolished as part of the half-acre Edwin-Colne Road redevelopment plan in 1976 and 1977, together with a cluster of houses and factories that extended back from Heath Road to Colne Road. According to newspaper reports in 1977 the owner of nos 4–2, then a furniture retail showroom and offices, was reluctant to vacate the premises.

An extra floor, with dormer windows in the roof, has been built on no. 6, bringing it to the level of the new buildings as well as giving some visual continuity. It is now a greyish-pink and again empty. Sadly, while the new but bland brick and dormer-roofed offices, with their dark ground-floor recesses, may perhaps be more functional, they are certainly not very attractive for such a prime historic location. United Biscuits was here until recently. However, one improvement is certainly to the traffic island – which was a typical sterile 1960s contribution to the Twickenham townscape.

Heath Road looking towards The Dip, with the new brick and dormer-roofed office building already completed, 1970s. The first of the old original cottages (no. 194) beyond was briefly a doctor's surgery, next to which (no. 192) was the third of Blay's of Twickenham shops (officially, C.A. Blay Motorcycles). Blay's slogan used to be 'Known the World Over', which may contravene the Trades Descriptions Act nowadays. The road then dropped down beneath the railway bridge, while the pedestrian walkway (with the railing on the right) continues at the same level through a separate tunnel, emerging into Heath Road proper. After heavy rain 'The Dip' often flooded, causing traffic chaos and bus delays.

The cottages are still there in 2006, just about recognisable by the roof-line, but the surgery is now Twickenham Green Cars, a taxi-hire firm. Although the other two Blay's shops still exist (one immediately opposite and the other at no. 38 The Green), this one has gone, converted into a private house, while new town-houses have been built on the space between Heath Road and Colne Road, next to what used to be 'The Arches'. In the 1950s and early '60s, Blay's had a workshop and yard under the railway bridge, facing onto Colne Road, opposite P. Chapman & Son's shop. Now the entire triangle and arches are used by Neal Chapman for his garden centre. It was a dark, oily, ramshackle place, where my mother's brother, Uncle George – who I remember as a tall, thin, silent man – worked for many years as a mechanic.

Heath Road, looking towards Lion Road and the Red Lion public house, during the 1981 Twickenham Festival parade. The shops visible in the background are no. 164, A. Boyall, hardware and ironmongery, and no. 162, Frank Sneller's, estate agents.

The Red Lion as it looks now, viewed from across Lion Road towards the railway bridge and The Dip. With its trees, cycle racks, bollards and new paving this is an improvement on how it used to look.

No. 75 Lion Road, on the corner of Albert Road. I can now confirm this was a beer-house known as the Alton Arms from 1884–1960. The trade directory for 1940 listed it to one Frederick Caley, a 'beer retailer'; a greengrocer's was located on the opposite corner, at no. 77. Apparently it was then an off-licence until 1969, although searching the directories for the 1960s in the Local Studies Library I was unable to find any business listed for this address. Certainly by the time this photograph was taken sometime in the 1970s, and despite the shop façade, it had already ceased to be a business.

Both the former corner shop and the houses visible in Albert Road have been renovated and 'improved' – a process that had already begun even in the 1970s. The fences, box-like office, yards and gateways (the sign read 'Elliotts Removals') along Lion Road have been swept away for new housing. The shabby brick and concrete rendering of the original shop has been painted over a clean white, and a low front wall defines the property boundary with the street. Unlike the terrace houses, the upstairs windows are still in character with the building, which has also retained something of its previous shop-like appearance, except that the original shop doorway has been blocked up.

Heath Road, Clifden House, built in 1886, demolished in 1974, with the entrance to Clifden Road on the left. Old photographs from the late nineteenth century show Heath Road still lined with trees and big elegant houses behind high walls. Unfortunately nothing of this charming scene has survived. Indeed, Clifden House was the last survivor from that time.

UK House, built on the site of Clifden House, now the UK Civil Service Benefit Society, with Dexter's estate agents and Möben Sharps and Dolphin kitchens, bedrooms and bathrooms on the ground floor. A functional box, nothing else. The maple tree is the only feature to appear in both photographs.

A view of Railway Approach into Station Yard, from the London Road bridge, during the demolition, c. 1977. The shop signs read Fishbourne & Randall; Café (name unknown); W.J. Bridger (function unknown, possibly a confectionery/newsagent's); and the ground-floor shell of the Warehouse.

Diligent research by Luke Denison at the Local Studies Library unearthed that no. 11, Fishbourne & Randall, had been a barber's shop for seventy years, and for the last forty-six years until January 1974 run jointly by Cyril Fishbourne (who had taken over the business from the previous proprietor, Mr Fred Cross, in 1926), and Arthur Randall, who had joined two years later. The Warehouse had previously been a furniture depository for Phelps, before becoming a community workshop, arts centre, play centre for children, and a musical and theatre unit. However, in 1973 it was deemed 'structurally unsound', which limited activities to the two ground-floor shops. This parade of shops can be recognised from a 1905 photograph, when Railway Approach was still known as Station Road. Queens Road and the Albany public house can be seen in the right-hand background. According to local residents Geoff Dadswell and Ken Elmes, between the 1950s and early '70s, this parade of shops was a diverse mixture of cafés, fish and chip shops, sweet shops (one of which also sold second-hand bicycles), small offices, a car accessory shop, a print works and paper bag factory, a furniture depot and a barber's of course, and at one time the town's smallest public house.

Opposite above and below: The massive bulk of Bridge House now obstructs the same view from the London Road bridge. While the Station Yard car park and the Albany, Pub & Dining Room are still there, the old shops seen above, in Railway Approach, have now been replaced by a parade of nondescript town-houses, with walled gardens and off-road parking.

Above and below: Shelley's estate agents, 2A Railway Approach, looking towards London Road, with Regal House in the background, when the shops opposite were being demolished in 1977. Shelley's had occupied this Victorian building for nearly sixty years (it was known locally as 'Shelley's Corner'), before finally moving to new offices next to the police station in London Road in 1980, prior to the site being redeveloped. Again, I am indebted to Luke Denison for this information. It is possible that this wedge-shaped building was originally a private house.

Even the road layout of the junction of Railway Approach with London Road is slightly different today, wider and nearer to the Cabbage Patch public house, while the old Shelley's site is now the massive Bridge House, part of which is occupied by the Inland Revenue. Bridge House now dominates this view, while Regal House has had a blue-tinted makeover, and its roof now sprouts communications aerials and antennae.

Old St John's Hospital, on the corner of Amyand Park Road (left) and Oak Road. Founded in about 1880 by Elizabeth Twining (of the Twining tea family), and incorporating the eighteenth-century Amyand House, it was briefly known as the Twining Hospital. After a brief closure due to financial reasons during the 1880s, it continued as a cottage hospital for another hundred years, until 1988. Excavations carried out in 1994 by the Museum of London Archaeological Service revealed traces of Roman and pre-Roman occupation in this area.

Sadly the delightfully ad-hoc, chaotic work-a-day appearance of the previous picture has given way to an almost immaculate orderliness. By 1993 the building had become derelict and vandalised, despite its Grade II listed status. It was extensively renovated and reopened in 1995 and is now part of the South West London and St George's Trust, initially specialising in the treatment of elderly patients with depression, dementia, Alzheimer's and schizophrenia, but now extending to those with behavioural difficulties – operating both as a day hospital and long-term care. However, despite the ever-growing need for such psycho-geriatric and mental health institutes in our modern age, the unit is again threatened with possible closure.

London Road from Holly Road, 1970s. No. 24, the old post office, was built in 1908 in what is known locally as the Christopher Wren Hampton Court style; next to it is no. 22, Moore's Self Service grocery and provisions. The old public house seen on the left corner of Holly Road, already boarded-up prior to demolition, was apparently the Grosvenor Arms, closed 1969, not the Duke of York, as I had previously believed. On the right is the side of no. 27, probably still Charrington's Heating Service.

In 2006 Christalz Wine Bar occupied the corner of the new Allied house building, seen here which was once the old public house. Opposite, 24 London Road, the old post office had become The Sorting Room – Lloyd's Bar. Next door, what was formerly Moore's, is C. Goode, pharmacy.

York Street, from London Road, 1970s. It was built in 1903, when London Road was widened and Church Road ceased to be the main road to Richmond. The Midland Bank can be seen on the near left. The shops in York Street were, from left to right, Alec Peters, opticians; Shoe Rebuilders; the Beryl Richards Organisation, sales promotions; and, on the extreme right, part of the Barclays Bank building that faces King Street.

The old Midland Bank building is now HSBC, while in York Street the shops are now: no. 10, Mystiq, a boutique; no. 8, Smiley Blue; Timpson, locksmith; and Chase Buchanan, estate agent's; while Barclays Bank is still visible on the extreme right. The road layout of this junction is now different, with walled pedestrian traffic islands, seating and trees.

York Street, looking towards Arragon Road, 1970s. The shops are, from left to right, no. 49, Bonnie Curls, hair fashion; no. 51, Desmond Cosmetics and Climax Cleaners (both already closed); no. 53, Lauderama, a self-service launderette; while on the other side of Arragon Road, at no. 55, is Shears, travel agent's.

The empty space in the foreground of the previous photograph is now the site of the Borough of Richmond Civic Centre (44 York Street), built in the 1980s, seen here on the right. All the buildings on the left of the earlier photograph have been demolished and replaced by new offices, 49–53 York Street. Dal Corsaro, a restaurant and pizzeria, now occupies the corner of Arragon Road.

Church Street from Church Lane, 1970s. St Mary's Church wall is on the right; while on the left is what since 1963 had been a low-walled car park (capacity fifty cars, once the site of the Two Sawyers Inn, later a cycle shop), which faced onto Church Street. In Church Street, from left to right, was no. 4, Burton Engineering; no. 3, Arragon House; and no. 2, then St Mary's Parish Rooms. The white tower in the background belongs to the old Gas Board showroom on the corner of Arragon Road and York Street.

The rather shabby old car park has been redeveloped as new houses in Flood Lane, with a landscaped shopping precinct. Next to 3 Church Street (Arragon House), and to the right, what was no. 2 is now the council-run Off the Record Counselling Services.

Church Lane, looking towards The Embankment, 1970s. The old Mission Hall, the roof of which is on the left behind the wall, was built in 1869, originally as an annexe to St Mary's Church. It later served as a private residence, school and scout hall. The building on the right (now 25 The Embankment) was built in about 1720, and was later in the eighteenth century the property of Thomas Twining, the tea merchant, who also owned Dial House (now the Vicarage).

The old Mission Room building has become the Mary Wallace Theatre, home to the Richmond Shakespeare Theatre for the last twenty-five years. The Mission Hall itself is now the auditorium, while the dressing-rooms were once a waterman's cottage, and what was once a courtyard is now the foyer. No. 25 The Embankment was originally acquired in 1994 to be Twickenham Museum, which eventually opened in 2000.

Eel Pie Island, from The Embankment, 1970s. In 1983 part of this boatyard was sold to a consortium and became two separate companies, Eel Pie Island Slipway and Eel Pie Island Marine.

Apart from the background trees of the nature reserve, almost everything in the previous photograph has gone. Between 1983 and 1996 the sheds were used by artists, craftsmen and boat-builders. Then, in November 1996, the two sheds nearest the woodland burnt down, apparently in mysterious circumstances, and have only recently been replaced by the present structures, which are advertised as 'offices/studios/workshops'. The present owner hopes to revive and reinvigorate not only Eel Pie Island's musical tradition but also that of the small workshops, studios and facilities for boat-building that flourished here before the fire. Desolation and dereliction have given way to activity and bustle.

The Eel Pie Island boatsheds, but viewed slightly to the west of the previous picture, about midway between the wooded nature reserve and the footbridge, 1970s. Again there is already a dismal air of dereliction about the place: the metal rusting, slipways overgrown. The island was originally known as Twickenham Ait or Parish Ayte (variations on an old English word meaning 'island'), but apparently the eel fishing tradition stretches back to before the Norman Conquest.

Both the old metal shed and its neighbour have survived, although the façade of the latter has been altered and now has glass windows on the upper floor. The blue and white building on the left belongs to Eel Pie Island Slipways Ltd. New housing has been built on the right, in the direction of the footbridge. Although proposed as long ago as the late nineteenth century, this bridge, finally linking the island to the mainland, was only constructed in 1957. During the late 1960s visitors still had to negotiate a sort of turnstile gateway before finally gaining access to the island – which then mostly comprised wooden chalets and small bungalows. Despite notices warning motorists that the area was liable to flooding, there were always plenty of cars parked there, and with spring-tide those that were not moved in time often finished up under as much as 2ft of water.

Eel Pie Island Hotel, viewed from the Surrey towpath, August 1970. Built in 1830 to replace the White Cross, an earlier, small inn, it went from being something of a middle-class tourist attraction in the nineteenth century to a venue for tea dances in the 1920s and '30s, until eventually it became first a jazz club, then, from 1962 to 1967 a blues and rock music venue and site of the Crawdaddy Club. As such it saw live performances by many of the great bands and performers of the period, including Cyril Davies, The Who, The Rolling Stones, John Mayall, Eric Clapton and Long John Baldry. Forced to close in 1967, it saw a brief resurrection in 1969. Pete Townsend, of The Who, lived in one of the eighteenth-century houses on The Embankment during the 1970s and '80s, and had a small recording studio on the island itself.

Eel Pie Island Hotel, again viewed from the Surrey towpath, during its final demolition, June 1971, following a mysterious – but no doubt very convenient – fire. Although the wooded nature sanctuary still survives at either end, almost all of this south-facing Surrey-side of the island now comprises (almost identical) modern housing and their moorings.

3
THE HAMPTONS

I spent my early teens living in Hampton Hill, first on Windmill Road, then Cross Street, before moving back to Teddington. To me, living there in the early and mid-1960s, it seemed an incredibly boring place. As with Teddington, although geographically we were in the London Borough of Twickenham, and later that of Richmond upon Thames, the feeling was, instead, that of a small semi-urban village, with London itself still only starting at, say, Chiswick or Barnes, or even Hounslow.

Of course this was an illusion, quickly shattered once you went further along the Uxbridge Road, where eventually the feeder-road from the M3 motorway ploughed its way through what was left of Hanworth and connected – by what became known as the Apex Flyover – with the Great Chertsey Road. From here on – all the way to Feltham and Heathrow – suburbia ruled supreme, and the fleeting glimpses of a former rural existence were being either systematically tamed or snuffed out.

It is perhaps most noticeable in Hampton Hill, and especially old Hampton, just what has been so quickly and quietly lost in the last thirty or forty years. John Sheaf, of the Borough of Twickenham Local History Society, and a long-time resident of Hampton, kindly helped supply much of the historical information about the local houses and shops, and one thing became very apparent from such research: the steady disappearance of the small community shop, a process that perhaps started even before the Second World War.

Once, Thames Street, Church Street and Hampton High Street had many small shops, but now almost all have gone, and the centre has shifted away from the heart of the old village to Station Road and around the railway station itself. Although the Bell and the Jolly Coopers in the High Street have survived (and outwardly they are almost unchanged), the two long-standing public houses/hotels, the White Hart and the Red Lion, have closed and been converted for residential or commercial use. Preservation of so much of old Hampton goes hand-in-hand with conformity – the individuality of shops; street façades; picturesque old buildings giving way to orderliness.

Hampton Hill is certainly more vibrant and exciting – with its restaurants, wine bars, pavement cafés, theatre and computer shops – but what has been lost are what I call the 'real' shops: the television repair shop; the grocer's; the butcher's (of which it is claimed at one time there were seven, although I can only remember four); general stores; ironmonger's and hardware stores; the small engineering companies and back street workshops; the quaint tumbledown cottages, corner shops and working-class pubs.

Throughout Teddington, Twickenham and the Hamptons there *are* improvements – in better and more attractive street-lighting, paving, landscaping and the planting of trees – but so much too has been needlessly lost or desecrated. This is not just a blanket cry for conservation. The extravagant, over-the-top Victorian architecture, the brown- and red-brick houses and shops may not always have been particularly beautiful, or even always very functional, but they were English – our unique vernacular style. What is most disappointing about much of the twentieth-century 'international modernist' urban architecture is, not just that it is so often bland and ugly, but that it could be anywhere. It transcends tradition, local building materials and styles so that, architecturally, everything and everywhere looks the same. The wonderful diversity that distinguishes, not just the different regions within Britain, but British architecture from that of France, Germany, Italy, Spain or central Europe . . . all that is lost.

Good design and conservation can go hand-in-hand. We can have our old buildings and streets and still enjoy the amenities and benefits of the modern world. Ugly urban construction and the inhuman scale of tower-blocks – sadly features that have already invaded the town centres of Teddington and Twickenham – affect our moods, thoughts and actions.

Nos 40, 38 and part of 36 Church Street, Hampton, with the White Hart public house in the background, 1970s. These cottages are over two hundred years old and appear on a map from 1826. The present White Hart was rebuilt in 1901, but an earlier building dates back to the eighteenth century, and at one time, before 1780, it was called the Six Bells – apparently after the six bells installed in old St Mary's Church in 1679. In 1773 it was purchased by David Garrick, the actor, who lived at nearby Garrick Villa, located on Thames Street. It is said that the dubious sport of bear-baiting was still held here as late as 1818.

The old White Hart is no longer a public house, but is now White Hart House, 70 Church Street, having been converted into residential apartments in 2005. With no off-road garages, parking is obviously a problem for residents. The cottages from the previous picture have survived relatively unscathed.

Nos 68, 66 and 64 High Street, Hampton – known locally as The Triangle, 1970s. According to John Sheaf of the Borough of Twickenham Local History Society (BOTLHS) no. 68 was Newport's General Store in the 1920s and, from at least 1931 until perhaps the early 1970s, was owned by a Sydney George Germany (S.G. Germany & Son, greengrocer). It had been a pastry shop. Then it became The Pantry, which had been a small delicatessen, selling exotic foreign foodstuffs, until eventually it closed in the 1990s. The central doorway of the old greengrocer's had already been sealed up and converted into an arched window, and it was to be converted into a house in 1996. One local informant told me that next door was once a fishing tackle shop, which according to John Sheaf was Wm Griffiths, sports outfitter, from 1931 until at least the mid-1950s. By the 1970s it had already been converted into a house.

No. 64, on the right, perhaps already closed and no longer a shop, despite the window, had been Albert E. Roberts, coal merchant, in 1931, but by 1953 the property was in the name of E. Roberts, a widow or son perhaps.

By 2006 much of the tiny, village-green-like grass triangle has become the inevitable car-parking space, although the trees are still there, and a circular metal seat has replaced the old wooden one. There are no traces of the former shops, as both have been converted into houses; the arched-window of no. 68 is again a front door. The square-paned Dickensian ground-floor window of the middle house has been replaced.

Ivy House, 78 High Street, Hampton, with no. 80, the hair stylist's on the left, which was built in what was once the front garden of the neighbouring Hope Cottage, 1970s. Ivy House is probably late nineteenth century in origin, as it does not appear on an 1863 map of the area.

The shop was converted into a small house in about 1991. There is a local story that a covenant specified it could only be used as a hairdresser's. The concrete street-light has gone and a traffic island has appeared instead; while the enclosed wall of Ivy House is now opened to a small courtyard, obviously used as a parking area. Although the red brick of the main façade is the same, the grey, rather dingy, pebbledash is now painted white, and there is a blue plaque commemorating the computer pioneer and mathematician Alan Turing (1912–54), who lived here from 1945 to 1947.

Old Farm House, 67 High Street, Hampton, opposite Douai Grove, 1970s. Not to be confused with the Old Farm House, once located in Old Farm Road and part of the Hampton Nursery Lands, this may also date back as far as the seventeenth century, or even late sixteenth century, although it was much altered over the years.

The elegant white of the 1970s photograph has given way to a peach colour in 2006, and recently the name was changed to Bricana. Unfortunately local historians could supply no further information about this house or anything of its history. The hedge at the front and trees that can be seen in the previous picture, have gone; and the windows of the wing fronting onto the pavement have been made smaller, a small round window has appeared above the front porch. The first picture could still be a typical large eighteenth- or nineteenth-century farmhouse; the contemporary picture, on the other hand, might be any large middle-class house in the suburbs.

The delightful Dutch or Flemish-style Old Grange, 2 Church Street, Hampton, April 1970. It was built in about 1650. During the nineteenth century until 1910 it was a private girls' school.

The pale grey west façade is now painted white, and some unfinished touching-up to the Flemish-style gables awaits attention. Part of the elegant early eighteenth-century Orme House, 4 Church Street, also used as a private school in the nineteenth century, can be seen on the left.

Nos 6–2 High Street, Hampton, viewed from Thames Street, 1970s. Nos 6A and 6B were then still a newsagent, advertising Players no. 6, and, although the shop name is not clear, it was known as the Galleon. No. 4 is the Coffee Rooms, and no. 2 was the Tudor Rose restaurant, later the Casa Dino Italian restaurant. The building probably dates from the early to mid-nineteenth century.

After many years as a newsagent, no. 6 was converted into two houses in about 1981; 6A is now called Quince Cottage; while nos 4–2 are now the Riverside Indian Cuisine take away. Picnic benches have replaced the old wooden seat, but the black shutters seen on the upstairs window of no. 2 are the same in both pictures.

Part of the old Red Lion Hotel public house and restaurant can be seen on the left, with the entrance to the rear car park. The adjacent 3 High Street, which was occupied by G. Kingsbury & Son, originally as a motor and cycle works, and later as tyre storage from 1897 until 1962, is here seen vandalised and in the middle of demolition, in about 1981. Station Road can be seen on the right. The Hampton Society has access to an excellent, high-quality black and white photograph from almost the same time, in which the shop at no. 5 – here already demolished – could still be seen. Another photograph in the same series shows the complex of buildings behind these two façades – all of which was demolished.

Sadly the old Red Lion is no more, having been converted to commercial use, the façade renovated and the side entrance gone; it is now Geoff Howe Marketing Communications. The modern 3 High Street is now Heron Court, built in 1982. It was originally intended for commercial usage, but is now mostly residential, with office space on the ground floor.

Nos 34–40 Thames Street, with the red-brick side wall of the old 1897 fire station building in the distance, 1970s. The front façade of no. 40, nearest the fire station, appears to have been either black or chocolate-brown; no. 38 is white, and from the late eighteenth century until 1909 was the Crown Inn; no. 36 is lime-green, with a large lower window and a gated side entrance to the rear. For most of the twentieth century it was a greengrocer's shop.

The arched entrance, door and windows of the old fire station are still painted 'fire-engine red' in 2006. The cottages now have more subtle colours – a pale blue-grey, pinkish-grey pebbledash, and white. The second-floor bow-window of no. 36 has undergone a retro look in brown wood varnish, but the gated side entrance is gone, now part of no. 34, Ian Sherdan's bookshop, originally a grocer's or general store/off-licence, then a bookshop from 1982, soon, however, to close down, the last remaining shop in the row.

Nos 28–4 Thames Street, 1970s. No. 28 possibly dates from the eighteenth century. It was a hairdresser in the late nineteenth century, then a tobacconist until 1940. No. 26 also had several metamorphoses between the late nineteenth century and the early twentieth – first it was a fishmonger, later a boot-maker. Between the 1890s and the 1930s no. 24 was a coffee house, then a diner.

Today the distinctive protruding window of no. 28 has been repainted, but still has green frames. No. 26 was formerly a dark green but, like the rest of the parade, is now a uniform white. In the contemporary photograph the end of the parade can also seen. No. 24 was originally part of the Old Red Lion, which dated to the seventeenth century, that was demolished in 1908. A greengrocer's in the 1890s, it was the Chalet Tea Rooms during the 1920s and the Tudor Café in the 1950s. The corner of the Riverside Indian Restaurant, 2 High Street, and Ferry House, 20 Thames Street, can be seen in the distance, behind which is the tower of St Mary's Church.

Nos 6, 4 and 2 Thames Street, now River Cottage, The Feathers and Garrick Cottage respectively, built in about 1540, with the rebuilt 1831 St Mary's Church tower just visible in the background, and the Bell Hotel public house glimpsed beyond that. Although all had later rear and frontage extensions, the core building is regarded as the oldest surviving structure in Hampton. Originally a church house, it was later (until 1792) an inn, and then the site of a blacksmith shop located in the rear yard of the property.

Apart from the street furniture and increased traffic along Thames Street into the Hampton Court Road, the 2006 scene appears comparatively unchanged.

Another view of The Feathers in Thames Street and Garrick Cottage, seen from the direction of Hampton Court Road, opposite Garrick Villa, 1970s. The Studio, or 1 Church Street, was built in about 1922 when the old blacksmith's shed was demolished.

In 2006 Garrick Cottage is almost completely overgrown with ivy, and a new curved wall now encloses the corner of Church Street. The trees of the vicarage are still visible over the rooftops, but the rather ugly concrete street-lighting has been replaced, here apparently re-positioned so as not to obstruct this historic building. The vicarage roof and upper storeys are visible in both photographs – the entrance being in Church Street, opposite the Old Grange.

The junction of Park Road, Hampton Hill High Street and Hampton Road, 1970s. In those wonderful bygone days when businesses and even shop signs seemed permanent, the inscription over the entrance still reads 'Matthews Stores – 1895'. At the time of the photograph it was already P. & J. Do-It-Yourself Ltd.

In its latest incarnation the old Matthews Stores is now 120 High Street, Greenwood Furniture, but otherwise the building is comparatively unaltered – unlike the parade of shops on the west side of the High Street, which has undergone extensive alteration, and opposite, which is currently under reconstruction. F.W. Paine, undertakers, is still on the facing corner of Hampton Road, although most of the other shops in that parade have changed.

Nos 139–41 Hampton Hill High Street, just down from Cross Street and the Duke of Clarence public house, 1970s. No. 141 was then Garners, hair stylist. These two shop units had been hairdresser's since at least the 1940s. A couple named Betzman originally had adjacent but separate shops for women and men. A former Hampton Hill resident told me that for many years the small end shop unit, nearest the Duke of Clarence, was boarded up and empty. Eventually it was incorporated into Garners.

No. 139 is now Coopers estate agent's and 139A is Scruples hair salon. The attractive white painted façade of all three units has been stripped back to a somewhat unsightly mix of bare brown and red brick, although, surprisingly, the gate between Coopers and Stewart & Young has survived.

Nos 131–5 High Street viewed from the Park Gate cut-way, 1970s. No. 131 was then named the Park Gate Timber Co., and had been a timber business certainly as far back as the 1940s. At the beginning of the twentieth century the butcher T. Prudanes had been F.W. Paines, also a butcher, and which claimed to have been established in 1818. Prudanes had gone by 1978, and by 1985 was already Pickwick's Wine Bar. For many years nos 135–7 was a gentlemen's tailor and outfitter's, which may at that time have been named Marksman.

No. 131 is still the Park Gate Joinery Co., and the building has the same green and white decorative façade. At the time of this photograph, summer 2006, no. 133, what had been Monsieur Max, cuisine bourgeoisie, was undergoing extensive alterations and has since become a pizzeria. The exterior tiles of the previous photograph, which are over a hundred years old, have been removed. The old gate entrance to the rear had already disappeared. Nos 135–7 is now Stewart & Young.

Old cottages, nos 125–7 in the 1970s, with the curious plaque on the upper storey wall reading 'E.J.F. 1879'. I have not been able to discover who or what 'E.J.F.' was – perhaps the initials of the original builder or owner?

No. 129 is now Hampton Hill Dental Care. The gateway had already been filled in by 1985. Beyond that can be seen the Park Gate Joinery Co.

High Street from Windmill Road, 1970s. From right to left: no. 38, the Hampton Press, a small local printing company of long standing; no. 40, Hampton Hill post office, which occupied this site from 1835 to 1995, before moving to no. 58; and no. 42, V.J. Breeden's – Newsagents, Confectioner, Greetings Cards. The Breedens, with whom I was particularly friendly in the 1960s, lived in one of the new houses in nearby Cross Street but had moved away by 1986.

What was Breeden's Newsagents is now Taps News; while no. 40 is now Billy Basin, a hair salon.

Nos 36–2 High Street, again viewed from Windmill Road in the 1970s, with the Crown and Anchor public house visible on the right; it was rebuilt in 1907. From left to right the shops are Gaskins, a shoe shop, and another very old Hampton Hill business (the sign reads 'Quality Footwear'); next is Frederick J. Sully, grocer's and provisions; then Shillingford, the butcher's, dating back to the 1940s, here advertising 'Scotch Beef Only'. However, Shillingford had already gone by 1976, while Sully's had disappeared by 1980.

Nos 36–4, 2006: Attic; no. 32, Jovanni's Café; no. 30A, Click2Print, photographic printers; and Cartridge World beyond that. The Crown and Anchor later mysteriously metamorphosed into the Valiant Knight, and is now Joe's Bar and Restaurant, which specialises in Mediterranean cuisine.

No. 30 High Street, W. Johnson & Sons. Yet again, this had been an ironmonger's shop for many decades, but by 1985 it had been transformed into Hampton Hill Sports.

No. 30 is now Click2Print and Cartridge World. Nos 28A and 28 (not included in the original picture, and now the Parkside Café), is on the right.

Nos 22A and 22 High Street in the 1970s, M. Elliott & Son, butcher, and Shepherds, which, from the window display, sold souvenirs, pictures, dolls and bric-a-brac. Whereas most of the other shops in the High Street often have histories dating back decades, into the 1950s, 1940s or even pre-Second World War, and their communal trade clearly defined, Shepherds appears to have evaded the collective memory of locals. I have been unable to find out anything about it, not even when it ceased trading.

Again, now completely transformed, both old shops were combined to become no. 22, the Royal Elephant Thai Restaurant, and before this, by 1985 it was the English Revival Restaurant. Champion travel agency can be seen on the left.

No. 12 High Street, the Cavan Bakery Ltd, with part of Mrs Scrimshire, draper, on the right, 1970s. The old shop front with awning was painted a deep green. Tony Cavan bought and took over this bakery from a Mr Clarke in 1939.

The bakery has survived – and thrived (there is another shop near the Park Road/Hampton Road junction, and a third in Hampton) – but the green is now replaced by a shade of peach, and the shop front and sign have been updated. The freehold of the adjacent cottage is for sale with long-established local estate agency, Sneller's.

No. 10 High Street, with part of the Star public house on the right, 1970s. Despite the name over the shop being Mrs Scrimshire, it was owned by a Mrs A.C.F. Evans, and was a draper's and women's clothes shop. John Sheaf tells me that Florence Scrimshire was the original draper who owned the shop between 1931 and 1937.

Another rare old gateway. The outward appearance of the shop seems almost the same, while the Mrs Scrimshire name has also been retained, despite a change of ownership and business; it is now an antiques shop. However, not long after this photograph was taken, it had closed down. The Star has had a welcome makeover, but thankfully still retains many original features, elegance and character – an example that sadly is not always followed by breweries or pub chains elsewhere.

The Lady Eleanor Holles School, Burlington House, Uxbridge Road, 1970s. One of the most distinguished girls' schools in the country, originally established in 1711, which moved from Hackney, in east London, to its purpose-built site on Hanworth Road, on the other side of the Longford river, in 1936. Although originally a private house, this building was later used as a boarding-house for children whose parents worked abroad in the British colonies, and the Lady Eleanor Holles School continued this tradition from 1937 until it ceased taking boarders in the 1960s.

Burlington House, 177 Uxbridge Road, now the Junior Department of Lady Eleanor Holles School. Mrs Patricia White, the school archivist, tells me that, although various additions and alterations have been made over the years, the frontage has remained largely unchanged. The last major renovation was in 2003.

Briar House, Uxbridge Road, 1970s. Although I believe at one time this house was used by Richmond Council, I have not been able to discover anything else about it.

Briar House, 179 Uxbridge Road, 2006. Small improvements have been made and trees planted in the front area, but a new building is now visible in the background, an example of the steady in-filling by new houses or blocks of flats of the large gardens and once empty spaces throughout the borough.

The junction of Park Road with Uxbridge Road, still looking comparatively rural in the 1970s, with tall trees and open spaces. A wooden pavilion or summer-house can be seen at the rear of the house, and then there was open garden all the way to the Longford river. One can imagine the crows cawing in the upper branches of the trees and the trill of songbirds.

Hofer House, 185 Uxbridge Road, 2006. The same view today. The delightful trees that once softened the skyline are gone and replaced by new housing; the street-furniture has been modernised, with the addition of traffic-islands and mini-roundabouts; the old walls have gone or been truncated, replaced by wooden fencing, behind which are new bungalows and town-houses. Now, I suspect, you only hear the continuous rumble of traffic.

Old Farm Road, Hampton Nursery Lands, 1970s, looking towards All Saints' Church on The Avenue, the roof of which can be seen in the right-hand far distance. The house in the middle foreground is Gardinia Lodge, with Chatford, the red-roofed bungalow, immediately behind.

On the Ordnance Survey (OS) map for 1895, Oak Avenue is still called Hanworth Lane and Old Farm Road is just Farm Road – the farm itself (which dated from the seventeenth century, then named Newhouse) was located between Marlborough Road and Nightingale Road, and was eventually demolished in the 1960s. What had been the Tangley Park Farm estate was broken up in 1863, but even in 1895 almost the entire area between Old Farm Road and Hanworth was still open fields, with the nurseries clustered around what was later to be South Road, Broad Lane, and between Buckingham Road and Hanworth Road.

Twenty years later, on the OS map for 1915, not only had buildings such as Tangley House and what is now Houghton and Gardinia Lodge sprung up, but almost all the open space on either side of what was now already Oak Avenue is covered with greenhouses. The landscape had been transformed.

Many of the small chalet-bungalows on the south side of Old Farm Road date from the post-First World War period, having appeared between the 1915 and 1934 OS maps. Both the bungalow, Chatford, and Gardinia Lodge are still there, the latter now half-hidden behind trees, a neatly trimmed hedge and five-bar gate, but the upstairs bow-window (glimpsed in the 1970s photograph) has gone, although the one on the ground floor is still there. Apparently it was in danger of falling off! An extension was built about five years ago. Despite the massive developments, the road here is still semi-rural and unmetalled, with grass verges and plenty of trees.

A side view of Houghton or what is now 30 Oak Avenue, and the white Tangley House with its red roof behind, seen from Old Farm Road. Oak Avenue can be made out in the darker line of hedgerow and trees running from the left, going in the direction of Hanworth. The scene is still typically rural, considering that Hanworth, and even Sunbury, had already long since succumbed to the ugly blight of suburban sprawl and the ravages of the M3 motorway.

It is impossible to replicate the previous photograph as all the foreground between Old Farm Road and Houghton is now new housing, comprising the southern end of Fearnley Crescent, Hawley Close, Rumsey Close, Walker Close and Grogan Close. The new houses facing onto Oak Avenue and the first part of Old Farm Road are covered in dark wood cladding and set behind wooden fences and trees, so that, despite the high density of buildings, a semi-rural village atmosphere has been retained. Trees and wooden fencing now divide this estate from Old Farm Road itself.

What is now 30 Oak Avenue, then still part of the former Hampton Nursery Lands. With its hedge and rather grand gateway it could be the archetypal Edwardian farmhouse. Like its near neighbour, Tangley House, it must have been built between 1895 and 1915. In 1931 a nurseryman named Pascaud is listed as living here.

No. 30 Oak Avenue, also known as Houghton, 2006. The hedge has been replaced by a wall, and a new wing was built on the right several years ago; at first glance it resembles just another large, nondescript suburban villa. One local Hampton resident, Tony Hillman, has speculated that there is a possible connection between the house name, nearby Houghton Close, off Stewart Close, and a nurseryman named Houghton. Did Mr Houghton live here? I assumed that Houghton was a surname, but, according to John Sheaf, in the 1930s there was a nurseryman named Houghton Percy White, who had a nursery in Buckingham Road. To the left of the previous picture is now the southern end of Fearnley Crescent.

Tangley House, Oak Avenue, 1970s. This house is believed to date from the late 1890s (it does not appear on the 1895 OS map), and was once owned by William Henry Page, the eldest of the five Page brothers (all originally from Teddington) who from 1890 kick-started the growth of the horticultural business in Hampton. William Henry Page, whose Tangley Nursery was located in Buckingham Road, was especially influential, innovative and pioneering in greenhouse techniques. He was an esteemed member of the Royal Horticultural Society and President of the British Florists' Federation, and although staunchly Conservative in his politics, he was something of a local philanthropist. Ironically, it would be a Conservative Richmond Council that would be the most enthusiastic promoter of building on Hampton Nursery Lands. The Page nurseries continued until at least the 1960s. At the time of this photograph much of the land on the left, and beyond Tangley House itself, was still nurseries. The overall impression was semi-rural.

Hampton Nursery Lands, 1970s. Despite extensive enquiries the actual location is unknown, but it can only be Oak Avenue, perhaps Old Farm Road, or The Avenue. From a total of forty-five nurseries in 1939, by 1973 (when proposals were already being mooted by Richmond Council for the land to be developed for housing) there were only eight left. But even without this insatiable pressing demand for new London housing, the introduction of bulk refrigeration and cheaper air freight from the 1960s resulted in greater competition from the Channel Islands and Europe, and eventually, of course, as far away as Asia or Australia. Thus economics and housing, together with possible deterioration of the soil and a falling water-table, ultimately spelled the death of over a thousand years of agricultural tradition.

While we might reluctantly concede the inevitability of the demise of the nursery lands and the last bit of rural southern Middlesex, perhaps the greatest complaint – then as now – is the dreadful higgledy-piggledy street-plan and the bland quality of architecture and imagination that replaced it. Even time and new trees have not softened or concealed the awful truth. The Nursery development is a mess, a laboratory rat's maze of alleys; dead-ends; confusing, twisting, snake-like streets; with a belated and insufficient thought to community facilities, entertainment, leisure or transport; and everything looks the same. it is the epitome of everything that has gone wrong with British urban renewal since the 1950s,and which – when we look at what is being built now, thirty-five years later – is only marginally better today, despite the painful consequences of past mistakes.

Opposite: This photograph is taken from a little further back than the 1970s photograph, with Fearnley Crescent in the foreground, but the red roof and white façade of what was once Tangley House can still be seen, here screened by trees, 2006. However, the grass verge and crude asphalt pavement has gone; and now there are intrusive traffic signals and road signs. It is now just 34 Oak Avenue. Some years ago there was a threat to demolish and redevelop this site, with a major new road off Oak Avenue and housing, but fortunately that did not happen. The blonde woman, seen on the right of the 1970s photograph, was the first Mrs Groombridge, who, after our divorce, later bought a flat in Abbot Close, part of the new estates that were to be built off Oak Avenue on the left during the early 1980s.

The Embankment at Twickenham looking towards Eel Pie Island at high tide, c. 1977.

Afterword

Living as we do, surrounded by motor traffic, street-lighting, busy streets, housing and council estates, supermarkets and railway stations, it has always amused me visualise a wilderness England of muddy unpaved roads leading from forest to bleak heathland; of tiny linear villages whose entire population probably equalled no more than that of one of today's suburban streets; whose meandering swollen rivers and untamed streams overflowed their banks and regularly flooded the lowlands and surrounding meadows.

Once history moved at a snail's pace. Things changed but slowly, over generations, or even hundreds of years. The Romans came and went; the Saxons settled along the river highway, living in small villages surrounded by fields and meadows; the Normans built no castles in Middlesex, but presumably hunted here; then came the Tudor palace at Hampton Court, easily reached by boat from London, and the first of many grand houses that were to dominate the Middlesex and Surrey riverbanks until the nineteenth century. The villages remained small; and the flat, agricultural land remained predominately farmland. But then the railway came, and gradually the villages grew into towns, and eventually small towns become suburbs. Even in the early years of the twentieth century much of the region still appeared to be rural.

Not so a hundred years later. We have a love–hate relationship with the future. We are ambiguous about the past, and obsessed by progress, novelty, new ideas and styles – in architecture, civic planning, transportation, interior design, commerce and economics, technology and illusions.

Hampton Court Palace, Marble Hill House, perhaps the older or more interesting churches, the parks and gardens are preserved – even lovingly restored – as if in a time-capsule. But so much else is either swept away, neglected, changed out of all recognition, or survives piecemeal, often out of context with new surroundings. Despite a greater accessibility to information, photographs, books, computer graphics and museums, it becomes harder for us to imagine what the past really must have looked or been like. With each old house that gets demolished to build another bland block of flats or a car park; each church that gets transformed into a night-club, Hindu temple or Islamic mosque; each bit of woodland, pond, or meadow that gets gobbled up so that some property developer or politician becomes richer; each new supermarket that sucks away life from town centres, and small shops or stores go bankrupt – each slow steady transformation takes us ever further from not just our historical past but from our heritage and roots: what made us, and this particular spot, special and unique.

'Water nymphs' at the 1981 Twickenham Festival next to the South Stand at Twickenham Rugby Ground, which has since been demolished and extensively rebuilt.